D1493352

Virgin MoDERN iCoNS

IGGY POP

Acknowledgements

With very grateful thanks to Philip Dodd,
Lucinda Hawksley, Helen Johnson, Morse Modaberi
and to John Stickland, Gary Stickland and the staff of the
National Sound Archive for their help in the research of this book.

Nina Antonia began writing about music as a teenager for fanzines in her native
Liverpool. As well as writing regular articles for *Mojo* and *Record Collector*, she
has chronicled the life of Johnny Thunders in her 1986 book *In Cold Blood*,
dissected the career of The Only Ones in *The One and Only* (1996), and is
currently working on an unexpurgated biography of the New York Dolls.

First published in 1997 by
Virgin Publishing Ltd
332 Ladbroke Grove
London W10 5AH.

Modern Icons series conceived and developed
for and with Virgin Publishing Ltd by Flame Tree Publishing,
a part of The Foundry Creative Media Company Limited,
The Long House, Antrobus Road, Chiswick, London W4 5HY.

Modern Icons series © Virgin Publishing Ltd 1997
Text © Flame Tree Publishing.

ISBN 1 85227 698 3

A catalogue record for this book is available from the British Library.

Printed and bound in Italy by L.E.G.O. Spa.

Virgin MoDERN iCoNS

IGGY POP

Introduction by Nina Antonia

CONTENTS

INTRODUCTION

Iggy Pop emerged screaming from the nightmare wing of rock history. Unlike his contemporary, Alice Cooper, Pop's shock treatment was for real, and he scorned the props of fake blood and chickens for a self-harming stagecraft that often involved him razoring his chest with broken bottles and smashing his teeth against microphones. Pop was the first rock musician to make living-suicide a career option and it's nothing short of miraculous that he managed to survive through to his fifties.

Legend has it that early on in the pursuit of his vocation, the Ig came by a pair of his hero Jim Morrison's black leather trousers – by slipping into his leathers, Iggy summoned up the same dark spirits that had possessed The Doors's frontman. Although Iggy metamorphosed into a much rawer performer, his

voice shares a certain crooning resonance with Morrison's, peppered by numerous animal howls and growls. Further traces of tonal similarity can be found with Pop's bad seedling, Nick Cave.

Iggy came kicking into the world on 21 April 1947 and was raised in a trailer park just outside of Ann Arbor, Michigan. In late 1966 he avoided getting drafted to Vietnam by camping it up in front of officers at Fort Wayne and flashing his cock, a gesture he would later regularly employ on stage. By the time he failed his audition for 'Nam, Pop was an ingénu on the local scene, having played drums with covers band The Iguanas, who took to calling him Iggy. He tagged on the surname Pop, not because he or his music was particularly popular, but in homage to neighbourhood junk fiend Jim Popp.

After The Iguanas, Pop joined The Prime Movers, among whose ranks he found himself a protégé in Scott Asheton (aka Rock Action),

who he taught to play drums by beating on huge gallon oil cans with hammers. Inflamed by Asheton's heavy tribal rhythms, Iggy set about getting his own band together. He enlisted the new drummer's equally manic brother Ron on bass and the band debuted as The Psychedelic Stooges at a private party in October 1967. The line-up was finalised at the end of the year with the addition of Dave Alexander. Iggy was able to ditch his Hawaiian-style sit-down guitar, Ron picked up lead guitar and Alexander took over bass duties. These Stooges would later be hailed as one of the most influential cult bands of the decade and prefigured the punk movement at a time when being called a punk was the ultimate in jailhouse put-downs.

Advancing like a missing chapter of transvestite Hell's Angels, with Pop wearing cute little maternity frocks and Ron Asheton developing a penchant for Nazi regalia, the band began assaulting audiences with their brutal electric cacophony. Ten Years After, The

Flying Burrito Brothers and The Faces were but a few of the acts to step out gingerly onto a debris-strewn, blood-splattered stage after their support act, The Stooges, had finished the first set. In 1969, Danny Fields, the innovative head of publicity at Elektra (the Doors's label), who had arrived in Detroit to negotiate a contract with MC5, was introduced to The Stooges by the '5's guitarist Wayne Kramer. Unlike the MC5, their politically minded and politically motivated cohorts, The Stooges had no social agenda whatsoever, but their genuine nihilism appealed to

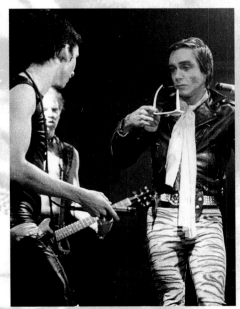

anyone who gagged on the word 'hippy'. Danny Fields bravely offered them a deal.

The band recorded their eponymously titled debut in less time than it took God to create the world, which probably accounts for the album being such a base and scary effort, as the whole thing was completed in just four days, well before any love, peace or understanding could be developed. Produced by the Velvets's John Cale, the album reached Number 106 in the US charts and featured two songs, 'No Fun' and 'I Wanna Be Your Dog', which the Sex Pistols would go on to adopt. A year later, Iggy and The Stooges went to LA to record their second album, 'Fun House'. A glowering seven-track slab of free jazz terror, 'Fun House' contains seething renditions of 'Down On The Street', 'Loose', 'TV Eye' and 'Dirt'. Unfortunately, the vice-president of Elektra failed to appreciate The Stooges' demented disk and jettisoned the band back to the street where they'd been found.

As the Sixties waned, so did a generation's aspirations. The three J's – Janis Joplin, Jimi Hendrix and Jim Morrison – all checked out to meet their makers. The Manson gang put a murderous curse on Hollywood, and Altamont climaxed in bloodshed. Downers replaced acid in the narcotic popularity stakes, so much the better to blot it all out. By the early Seventies Iggy and practically all of The Stooges had succumbed to the oblivion of heroin addiction, pawning their equipment to fund

growing habits. The carefree days of Iggy launching himself onto his audience after two tabs of acid had become distorted into a junkie death trip. Eventually the original members of the band drifted apart, leaving Iggy and arch-guitarist James Williamson to keep up a semblance of activity, even if it just involved nodding out in a ratty basement.

Some kind of salvation came in the form of Pop aficionado David Bowie and his then manager Tony DeFries. After signing with Bowie's management, the MainMan company, Iggy secured a two-

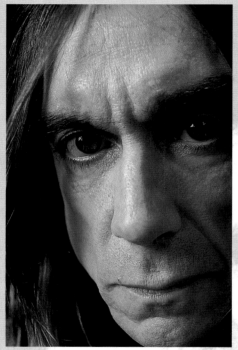

album deal with CBS and reformed The Stooges. Iggy and his henchmen were exiled to London to record their third album, 'Raw Power'. Nauseated by the UK's prevailing glam scene and teeny-bop acts, The Stooges honed their proclivity for hatred while working in the studio. The result was one of the most malevolent albums of all time, eight songs of wrack and ruin from 'Death Trip' to 'Penetration' and 'Search And Destroy', Iggy cooing and moaning halfway between orgasm and death. One hot summer's night in July 1972, the low-life, low-rent district of London's Kings Cross was flooded by freaks en route to the theatre where Iggy and The Stooges were making their live UK debut. By all accounts the show was a shattering experience, Iggy with his Nijinsky physique burning up the stage like a flame exhaled by Satan. (It's worth noting that a young John Lydon attended the gig.)

The band returned to the States where 'Raw Power' had strangled on the vine at Number 182 in the charts. Although a fourth album was on the cards, more energy went into fights between the band members and arguments with management and CBS. The recordings that had been completed were shelved, but Iggy, as usual, remained undeterred by such trivial irritants as these major obstacles and began to plan a lengthy US tour.

Pop had used up most of his $100,000 record advance on a suite at the Beverly Hills Hotel, where he'd lewdly propositioned a once-famous actress. With the cash gone, he hit on Danny Sugerman, The Doors's former office boy, for shelter and drug money. Sugerman spent his time bailing Iggy out of a myriad of unfortunate situations which included calming down one of Iggy's wealthy one-night stands after Pop had taken an axe to her daddy's Mercedes and convincing the local police department, who had arrested Iggy for impersonating a female, that The Stooges' frontman was actually harmless.

Iggy had never been of a particularly sound mind but now, as the tour revved up, his brain was reeling to an orchestra of self-hate. The rest of the band were also pushed to the limits of their mental capacity, Scott Asheton declaring that by refusing to change his clothes he was getting closer to God. The dates came to a horrific close in February 1974, at the Michigan Palace in their home base Detroit. Earlier on the day of the gig, whilst being interviewed on the radio, The Ig had broadcast a challenge to a neighbourhood gang, The Scorpions – one of whose members had permanently scarred Pop at a previous gig – to come down to the Palace and do their worst. The Scorpions picked up the thrown gauntlet and the last ever Iggy and The Stooges show proved to be a watershed in barbarity: Iggy asking, no begging, to be beaten to a rotten pulp by the gang who viewed him as nothing more than a moving target waiting to be hit. Time and again Pop baited The Scorpions, but to his disgust he came out of it alive.

After this cataclysmic performance, The Stooges split up for good and Iggy had no place left to go but into a mental hospital. David Bowie was reported to have been his only visitor. Iggy finally gave up trying to die and with Bowie's help, began what was to become a successful solo career. Pop convalesced on an unlikely diet of valium, golf and methadone and took to wearing matching flat caps with Bowie which made both of them resemble rather effeminate

Hovis boys – no one said recovery was going to be easy!

Iggy relocated to Berlin where he restored himself amongst the remnants of ruin and rebirth. He rehearsed a band in the former screening room of Fritz Lang and the German Expressionist school of film makers, their sombre influence seeping into Pop's next record, 'The Idiot', released in March 1977. The end of the same year was marked

by the release of 'Lust For Life', a classic album that many consider to be Pop's definitive statement.

He toured Europe wearing a horse's tail but this was no little pony act. In England he played to packed venues where enraptured punks flocked to see him, and the press dubbed Pop 'The Godfather of Punk'. The Good Lord and parental status had nothing to do with it. Iggy had always been his own man, a unique performer affiliated to no one, but he did cross the line in performing standards and was rewarded by a hail of spittle from the UK punks for his pioneering activities.

Through the late Seventies and mid-Eighties, Iggy continued working; however, the spectre of addiction loomed and leered as it regained its hold on Pop. He would later be alluded to as a motif of the heroin world in the screen adaptation of Irvine Welsh's book *Trainspotting*, from the opening sequence which is propelled along by 'Lust For Life', to a poster of Pop on a bedroom wall.

It wasn't until the release of 'Blah, Blah, Blah', and a top ten single, 'Real Wild Child' in 1987, that Iggy truly cleaned up and hit full stride again. The modern primitive was back with a new regime, and critical acclaim and respectable sales followed.

Iggy however, remains untameable. It was the rest of the world that had to catch up. Although Pop has matured in both spirit and musical style, he retains an indomitable candour and a tendency for

explicit behaviour that keeps him left field of mainstream, which is probably just the way he planned it. Iggy's unnerving, unique character has made him a natural casting choice and he can be found in a series of offbeat roles in films as diverse as Martin Scorsese's *The Color Of Money* and Jim Jarmusch's *Dead Man*, in which Pop excelled himself playing a hillbilly hag.

For all of his hard-won prizes, Pop chooses not to be captured by the likes of *Hello!* magazine, posing on a leopard-skin bed throw and discussing favourite interior designers, nor does he sip champers with the old boys' club of the rock aristocracy. Pop is always going to be the feral kid of Detroit – a trailer-born Tarzan swinging from microphones and beating his chest in time to the throb of drums. No matter how many times he's landed flat on his ass in the past, Iggy Pop has always got back on his feet, pummelled his way to unheard extremes in the rock'n'roll jungle, and emerged grinning.

NINA ANTONIA

TO HELL AND BACK

Iggy Pop often gave the impression he was trying very hard to die, but his self-destructive streak always lost out at the final turn to some deep-rooted, primeval instinct for survival. Before the final cataclysmic performance by Iggy and his Stooges, he had barefacedly challenged a local Detroit biker gang to take him down. The cover of the bootleg album of that gig shows him lying spark out on the stage, as if his death wish had been answered, but it was not to be. In the months that followed he looked to drugs to finish the job, but however crazed, however reckless his lifestyle, Iggy Pop always came back from the brink. When he almost teetered over, he checked into a mental hospital – the best thing that could have happened to him. He had the space and time to heal, far from the feeding frenzy of Stooges Manor, the house that he and the band rented in Detroit, a male locker-room of excess, where they egged each other to go one step further, claiming a number of victims along the way. Seeing very few people while he was in the institution, possibly only David Bowie, who had been a Pop ally since 1972, Iggy convalesced, cleaning up mind, body and spirit, and emerged to start work with Bowie on his first post-Stooge offering, 'The Idiot'.

They went to Berlin to get away from it all. A new city with new prospects, somewhere where Pop felt that people weren't on his back all the time, where the local police weren't looking for a reason, any

reason, to bust his chops. Away from the studio he spent much of his time in quiet, calm reflection, a million miles from the public persona of a paranoid madman mutilating his own body. It was a time when he could find himself after exploring the darkest edges of his psyche. Despite later peeks over the chasm, and despite all the self-abuse, he has endured, and like Keith Richards, has become a talisman of rock'n'roll survival.

Ya nearly killed me
but ya missed again!
Iggy, on stage at the last Stooges concert, 1974

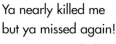

*By the time Iggy was admitted to the Neuro-Psychiatric
Institute in Los Angeles, he really had reached the bottom.
The few performances he gave were grotesque, and he was
living the life of a street bum, losing his self-respect and
mistreating his friends. According to some sources, the
police eventually found him in an incoherent mess under the
counter of a burger bar and gave him the option of prison
or psychiatry . . . .*

There are things I don't remember. I used to reach blackout
point really easily and still be walking around. I'd wake up
with bumps on the head, blood on my shirt and something
green coming out of my penis.
Iggy Pop, *The Guardian,* 1996

I only met my son recently, though he's nine now. Before that
I wasn't good enough. He didn't need a junkie, a pill addict,
or a slobbering quaalude idiot hanging around him.
Iggy Pop, 1979

I think he respected me for putting myself in a loony bin. He
was the only guy who came to visit me . . . . Nobody else
came . . . nobody. Not even my *so-called* friends in LA . . .
but David came.
Iggy Pop, *NME,* 1977, on David Bowie

Bowie and Pop formed an unlikely pairing. Ziggy and Iggy. Bowie was a long-term fan, once letting it slip that 'Jean Genie' was all about Pop. Theirs was a case of opposites attracting, meshing together, bringing to the relationship complementary talents and attitudes. Iggy said they were like blood relations, too close for comfort. There would always be arguments, but underneath there was enormous respect.

Bowie was kooky. That's the kind of person I tend to hang around with. I learned a lot from Bowie, about hard work and applied strategy.

Iggy Pop, *The Guardian,* 1996

It was like an old roué had taken an orphan from the streets to improve him.

Nico

I was not executive material like him. I couldn't do the things he seemed to do so well and so easily. Yet I knew I had something he didn't have and could never have.

Iggy Pop, *Mojo,* 1996, on Bowie

I hope Iggy's not dead, he's got a good act.

David Bowie, *Rolling Stone*

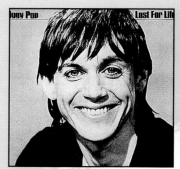

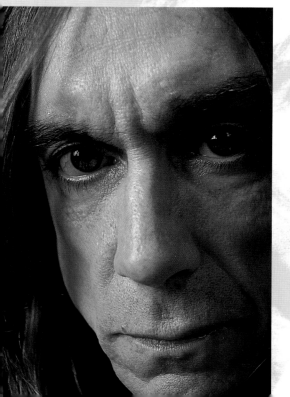

*Reviews of Iggy gigs, either in the Stooges' days or during his
solo career, invariably comment on the intensity of his
performance, that there is something driven at the heart of his
art, that he projects a sense of total commitment, of staying true
to himself, while all around him tastes and fads ebb and flow.
And so, when the mood is right – punk in 1976, grunge in the
Nineties – there he is, perfectly in tune with the times.*

I've been through it all. I've been the puppet, the arsehole,
the dupe, the junkie, and I've come through it and proved
I'm the equal to anybody you'd care to mention.
Iggy Pop

Sometimes I hate rock'n'roll, and sometimes I love it. Sometimes
I'm horribly depressed by it, and sometimes I'm ecstatically
happy. But I stay in it. I stay in it because I still believe, I still
have a strange naive belief that it is me . . . .
Iggy Pop, *The Face,* 1981

I never did feel rebellious; I was just someone who was
determined to do it right and do it my way. What I was
never able to do was attract people in positions of
responsibility in the industry to my way of seeing things.
Iggy Pop, *Sounds,* 1986

WE HAVE IGG-NITION

There are two Iggys. Or rather there is one Iggy and one James Osterberg. The creature we know as Iggy Pop was not conceived in some hellish urban spawning-ground, but in the ordered society of Ann Arbor, a forty-minute drive to the west of Detroit and home to the University of Michigan campus. His father taught English literature in a local school, his mother was an executive secretary, both hardworking, both 'arrow straight' in Iggy's words. The only notable oddity in their life was that they chose to live in a trailer park. The young James Osterberg, known as Jimmy, was by all accounts a pillar of his community. At high school he was president of the student council and held the vice-presidency of the debating society. He was voted most likely to succeed in ninth grade. But somewhere inside Jimmy's mind the seeds of extreme rebellion had been planted. They took a while to flourish. Even when Iggy started playing drums regularly, it was in the ranks of The Iguanas, a quintet of fresh-faced, neatly coiffed lads in matching jackets – the only malevolent note was the reptile that crawled across Jimmy's kit. This iguana would leave its mark as the source of Iggy's nickname. The band were good enough to turn semi-pro, supporting Motown acts like the Shangri-Las when they played in the neighbourhood. Shortly afterwards Jimmy invented Iggy, and from that point on the two sides of his character co-existed. James, lovable, thoughtful, articulate,

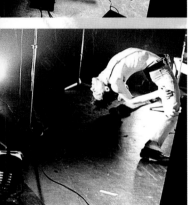

witty. Iggy, the scuzzbucket asshole, stoned and selfish, fickle and fiendish. The beauty was that James always knew where Iggy started and finished. Even when Iggy threatened to dominate and destroy both personalities, there was always the James Osterberg persona to retreat back into, a small haven of sanity, just so long as the physical entity that contained them both lived on.

My life as a child was very sheltered. It was an incredibly isolated environment. I never felt like the other kids anyway. I felt weird.

Iggy, *The Guardian, 1996*

Iggy's father was, according to Pop's later accounts, a highly strung, extremely shy disciplinarian. He didn't drink, never smoked and refrained from swearing, especially when ladies were present. He forced Iggy to sport a military-style haircut just like he did, and picked out his son's clothes for him. The pent-up frustration finally broke loose.

Jim is the smart, self-educated, undemonstrative individual. Iggy is the gut-level man of action. Jim wears specs. Iggy wears shades.

Roy Wilkinson,
Sounds, July 1988

I adore the hell out of my parents . . .
[but] I was sheltered, so what you ended up with by
the time I was eighteen was this guy screaming ready
to get out of high school, get out of home, dye his hair
platinum, wreck cars, chase girls and beat on drums.
When I played there was a mighty din – a set of
drums in a 50 by 10 trailer: the place would literally
shake! And they never complained, never once.
Iggy Pop, *Q* magazine, 1988

My words are important. They mean
something. They tell a story, my story, about
part of my life, meaning part Iggy Pop, part
James Osterberg, two separate, dual identities.
I'm quite in control of both my identities.
Iggy Pop, *The Face,* 1981

I think I am a little
different upstairs,
yeah . . . but so
are a lot of people.
Iggy Pop,
Sounds, 1986

The dark side of James Osterberg allowed those who didn't care or dare to follow his lead to get their vicarious kicks. Iggy acted out everybody else's fantasies of a life of excess, without having to endure the side-effects. Legend has it that in 1973 CBS wanted Iggy as a freakshow to take on Alice Cooper: Iggy convinced the head of the record company he was the right choice by clambering up on the conference room table, blind drunk, and delivering a note-perfect rendition of 'Shadow Of My Smile'. His sheer chutzpah won the day.

I was not the most butch, cool guy in my school. I was one of the poorest musicians in the crop in Ann Arbor at first. I did not have much talent, nor did I have a magnetic personality. I wasn't even particularly good-looking, but I wanted to do it. I had a desire to do it.

Iggy Pop, *Q* magazine, 1988

Stooge vocalist Iggy Osterberg leaps off the stage into the laps of surprised girls and plays a game of Reverse-rapo, taking off his shirt, pulling down his pants, then goofing on the girl and walking away. He has the potential to make Jim Morrison look like a tame puppy.

Eric Ehrmann, *Rolling Stone,* 1969

The part of myself I like best is the guy who would dare sing a song like 'Search And Destroy' in the era I did, in 1969, so soon after 'California Dreamin'; who said, Stick your flower power up your ass 'cos you're not sincere about it. Yeah, that's a side of myself I admire.

Iggy Pop, *Sounds,* 1986

Even before the Stooges recorded their first album in 1969, Iggy's stage presence had the power to disturb those who caught his act. Pop recalls that at their very first performance, a private party one Hallowe'en, everybody left in embarrassment. After the set, his friends approached Iggy, put their arms round him and asked if he had mental problems . . . .

I just started out with a big wild resolve that nothing would get in my way, nothing would bend me in half, nothing would take it from me.
Iggy Pop, *Sounds,* 1987

I'd created this character, Iggy, and it seems to be resonating well in the culture and people are believing all sorts of things about it. Yet if anyone hangs out for more than fifteen minutes, and gets to know me, I can't support that myth.
Iggy Pop, *Q* magazine, 1988

Obviously I am a genius, but that's just coffee to a cup. The right substance in the right place. If you wanna talk smart, I'll beat you in any mental game, not because of IQ but because of my will to win.
Iggy Pop, *Zigzag,* 1977

THE DUM DUM BOYS

After Iggy invented himself, he invented The Stooges. After playing for a while with the Prime Movers, a bunch of blues freaks, he headed over to Chicago to submerge himself in the city's blues culture. He returned to Michigan determined to start his own band, this time as lead vocalist, abandoning the drums. He got back in touch with an old friend, Ron Asheton, who'd been playing in a loose band called the Dirty Shames with his brother Scott and Dave Alexander. They'd all known Iggy since schooldays. The principal obstacle to their success was that none of them knew how to play their instruments. Iggy took them on anyway, and they got themselves a name: sitting around one day, talking, getting stoned, a re-run of The Three Stooges *came on TV, and The Psychedelic Stooges were born. As frontman, Pop then took on the job of teaching the others some musical skills. Just as The Clash's Paul Simonon would learn the rudiments of bass guitar in a few days, no technique threatened to spoil the raw energies about to be released. The sound they began producing was direct, aggressive garage rock. No frills, virtually no chord changes, lots of fuzz, plenty of distortion. They began to develop their own community, a male locker-room bunch of guys spending all their time together. They got their own house: it was like* Men Behaving Badly *on acid. Later the drugs would tear them apart, and envy and jealousy would*

intervene, but at the beginning there was trust and fun and togetherness, and the balance between Iggy upfront and Ron Asheton's power chords behind created a powerful alchemy. Within a year, that magic would entrance Danny Fields, an A&R scout for Elektra Records (the Doors's label), in Detroit to sign MC5. His first view of the Stooges: Iggy wearing a maternity dress, his face painted white, spitting at the audience.

Ron and I decided we wanted . . . a Real Band. With Real Soul. Literally, Fame and Fortune. While we went on to Oblivion.

Iggy Pop, *Zigzag,* 1970

41

*The Stooges' genius was in their mix of ineptitude and
a self-belief bordering on arrogance. They knew they
were crap and they simply didn't care. They were just
having fun. And over the relentless backing of the
band, Iggy could act out his own mini-dramas,
freewheeling wherever his mood swings took him.
You either understood where they were coming from
or looked on in disgust and extremely high dudgeon.*

Oh no, I've certainly heard this voice before, it's those
bloody Stooges. We worked with them in the States
and they were terrible. The singer is absurd, he swears
at the audience, and then throws himself into them.
You know this sort of thing really annoys me. I work
my guts out, and we all do to put over the best we've
got, and then we share a bill with somebody like this.
Maggie Bell of Stone The Crows, *Melody Maker,* 1970

Iggy, resplendent in silver hair, black lipstick, bare
torso and silver hipsters, mercifully restrained himself
from some of the wilder assaults on the audience that
have seeped their way into rock mythology, but the act
was an assault nevertheless. The Stooges are loud,
LOUD . . . They're really tight but highly monotonous.
Steve Peacock, *Sounds,* 1972, on The Stooges' UK debut

The reason The Stooges were unique was 'cos they couldn't play, man. That's why they started to come out with all this other shit, to get a reaction because no one gave a fuck about them. They just weren't good enough.

MC5 drummer
Dennis Thompson, *Mojo* 1996

MoDERN iCoNS – IGGY POP

There was already a definite scene in Detroit when the Stooges started out. The MC5 (Motor City Five) were the boss band; as figureheads of John Sinclair's White Panthers Party, they espoused a blend of revolution, sexual liberation and high energy rock'n'roll, and had run into some controversy over their use of obscene lyrics. The MC5 adopted the Stooges as their little brother band, but to many people they still seemed like no-hopers, sometimes even to their own lead singer.

A lot of what made me angry on stage came from how pissed off I was with the Stooges. They were such lazy bums! I was the worker in the band, and they wouldn't make an effort to be articulate or decent to people. They were way more extreme than I was; I was the moderating influence.
Iggy Pop, *Q* magazine, 1988

Great guys. But really they were hillbillies out of their element. They had nothing going for them.
One-time Stooge **Scott Thurston,** *Mojo,* 1996, on the original line-up

The picture on the cover of the album shows the Stooges to be four nice middleclass-kids-gone-wrong wearing brand-new synthetic leather jackets and pouting at the camera in a kind of snot-nosed defiance. They don't look all that bright.
Edmund O. Ward, *Rolling Stone,* 1969, on The Stooges' debut release

They're one hell of a rock'n'roll band, but I'll tell you, something awful funny must've happened to those guys when they were little kids.

Audience member **Ace Rickley,** *Rolling Stone,* 1970

Iggy said you had to be like a child to understand the Stooges, or rock'n'roll in general. The simplicity, the wildness and the abandon of their music, untainted by musical or intellectual posing, ensured that their influence would live on, even when the band collapsed. The lifestyle that accompanied their music, and that was an essential part of it, finally brought them down in a blur of drug-taking and lusty corruption. Dropped once by Elektra, they regrouped with CBS, but were fired after the record company reportedly found the Stooges had incurred an unaccountable expenditure of $500,000 in one six month period.

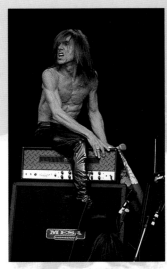

Just such an inescapable sound. You could tell they were being spontaneous, which was what made me realise it would be cool to make records. It was the sound of the record, too. Devastating. You followed the guitar as it snaked through all this noise and it really led you somewhere. At the same time, it was romantic – definitely as wild as youth gets.

Perry Farrell of Porno For Pyros, Q magazine, 1995, on 'Fun House'

We stepped into that vortex and showed them the vulgarity, the base side that they pretended didn't exist. Every day I would walk around very angry about the hypocritical things I saw going on around me. I kept my mouth shut about it because I wasn't in a position to question it verbally, and built it up into fuel for Stooges' shows.

Iggy Pop, Q magazine, 1988

Arguably they were the greatest rock'n'roll band ever. Iggy says that their singular achievement was to 'make people forget the 60s'. Indeed, if flower power *was* poisoned it was The Stooges' extreme brand of rock defoliation that was used in the process.

Ralph Traitor, Sounds, 1987

Who out there hates The Stooges?
Hands up who hates The Stooges.
Well, we don't hate you. We don't even care.

Iggy Pop, 1974, at the Stooges' last gig

SEX'N'DRUGS'N'ROCK'N'ROLL

● ●

Iggy, with and without The Stooges, became the most prominent citizen of rock'n'roll Babylon. He was the embodiment of the sex'n'drugs'n'rock'n'roll cocktail: it had existed before, but Iggy took it to new heights of exquisite pain and perfection. The myths that he created and which grew up around him may frequently be apocryphal. It doesn't really matter, because if only half of them contain a grain of truth, they are ample evidence of the licentious lifestyle that Iggy and the boys enjoyed at Stooge Mansions, the original Fun House that they rented on the back of Elektra Records's advance, a large white house on the corner of Packard and Eisenhower in Ann Arbor. This was the centre of their Stooge universe, a place with a reputation for attracting lots of beautiful women and lots of drugs. The kind of place where the guys would staple their female conquests' panties to the kitchen counter. Together they progressed down through the hierarchy of drugs. And wherever they went the Fun House went too, heading out to Hollywood for the recording of their second album, where they stayed in the Tropicana Hotel, cruising the Strip, discovering heroin, enjoying themselves in the company of actresses whose movies were strictly for adults only. By all accounts it wasn't a pretty sight, and not unexpectedly took its toll. Roadie/guitarist Zeke Zettner died as a junkie in 1975. Dave

Alexander, the bass player from the original line-up died the same year from pneumonia and alcohol abuse. The survivors could count themselves extremely lucky.

It took Iggy with 'Death Trip' to snap back a few heads and plunge us all into the abyss. Spinning recklessly down the spine of Manson's equation of death'n'sex being the final trip. The ultimate self-destruct orgasm.

Allan Jones, *Melody Maker, 1974*

MoDERN iCoNS – IGGY POP

The Stooges' sex symbol once claimed he was a virgin until he was twenty and even then had to be seduced by a predatory older woman, all of 25. Up until then he'd preferred his drums, he said, despite the promise of his school nickname: Horse Dick. Having discovered the possibilities, he decided to make up for lost time.

Iggy Stooge fondles the outlines of his fertile crescent. His shiny, skin-tight leather pants reveal a bulging basket of manhood . . .
Eric Ehrmann, *Rolling Stone,* 1970

I spent most of twenty years locked away in dark corners and shadows not really doing anything very glamorous – a lot of sex, which is interesting but not that glamorous.
Iggy Pop, *Q* magazine, 1988

The only thing Jim Morrison is into is displaying his cock so he can prove he still has one. When Iggy is on stage there's never any doubt.
Rita Redd, *Gay Power* magazine, 1970

When I did 'Raw Power' in London, I was celibate. Apart from one day when I saw this chick who was really *built*, walking her poodle down Fulham High Street and I thought, Mmm, this is interesting . . . I hopped on.
Iggy Pop, *Q* magazine, 1996

Iggy and the Stooges' exploration of drugs began with the regulation dope, then moved onto LSD. To get himself in the mood for performing Iggy would drop a couple of tabs of acid. An hour later it would have burnt out and he would be catatonic – that's why the Stooges only ever did short sets. Around the time of their second album the band got into coke and heroin. Drummer Scott Asheton says that was the sledgehammer blow. It was downhill from there on in.

When we first started it was really about a little marijuana and a lotta alienation. That was where we started from. What was good about us was that we had a certain purity of intention that was really good. I don't think we did ever get it from the drugs, I think they killed things.
Iggy Pop, *NME,* 1986

I took two grams of biker speed, five trips of LSD, and as much grass as could be inhaled before the gig. I found this concoction effective enough to completely lose my senses, and then before a gig we'd gather like a football team and hype ourselves up to a point where we'd scream 'OK guys, what're we gonna do? Kill! Kill!! Kill!!!' Then we'd take the stage.
Iggy Pop

I couldn't go on playing music with idiots who played their hair-dryers more than their instruments to audiences who were only interested in the size of my dick. It was the end.

Iggy Pop, *The Face,* 1986, on why he went into detox

I don't regret the drugs, because you can't. You can't start blaming things on certain chemicals.

Iggy Pop, *Q* magazine, 1988

53

Somehow, amid the drugs and the sex and the wildness of the performances, it was easy to lose sight of the fact that the Stooges were a rock'n'roll band. Iggy never did. Music was the driving force. It was why he'd started up the Stooges in the first place. Any other activity really was a bit of a distraction.

If a guy walked into this room right now
and handed me a cheque for a million dollars,
I'd only spend it all on forming a band.
Iggy, 1975

Indecent exposure. I took off my pants and went back on stage and started to do a striptease. I just sorta got crazed, I got out of hand. It was a little two bit thing not a big show.
Iggy Pop, *Zigzag,* 1970, after his bust in Romeo, Michigan

I've spent a few nights sleeping in cars and there have been a few problems, but all in all I'm much happier. I'm playing and that's the important thing. I think I've surprised the audiences who came to expect some kind of clown show. It isn't that at all, it's a rock and roll band.
Iggy, *Melody Maker,* 1973

THE SOUND AND THE FURY

Just as he pushed his lifestyle to the limits, Iggy Pop took performance further than any other rock star had. On stage, all the elements that were Iggy Pop came together. It was his domain, he had total control over what happened up there. He would flirt with the audience, twisting them round his own twisted little finger, giving them one moment a come-hither look, the next ignoring them. He could take their breath away with his physical abandon. He could have patented slam dancing, crowd surfing and stage diving. Inevitably bare-torso'd, his trousers low-slung or non-existent, he might hurl himself onto the stage floor, attack the audience (he claimed he'd always pick fights with much bigger people, guaranteeing he'd lose), or smear himself with peanut butter. Where Alice Cooper used props – electric chairs, gallows, boa constrictors – Iggy used his own body. Seemingly impervious to pain, at his most extreme he'd crush broken glass into his neck or cut himself with steak knives, while Ron Asheton, dressed in one of his many Nazi uniforms, laid into him with a whip. Even in his post-Stooge appearances the intensity was still there, taking out his aggression on defenceless amps or microphones, always moving, jumping, gyrating, disappearing up lighting rigs or out into the audience. A man in perpetual motion, like a hyperactive teenager. All his career Pop has caught the mood of mixed-up kids, screwed-up teenagers

overflowing with adolescent energy and a surfeit of unsated hormones. And like a lightning rod his energy could stir up negative forces: provoking a response of anger, violence and hate.

There are basically three kinds of people who 'perform'. There are those who do it naturally, those who desperately want to possess that ability but don't have that touch, and there are those who want to and don't give a damn either way. I'm part of the last category.
Iggy Pop, 1975

57

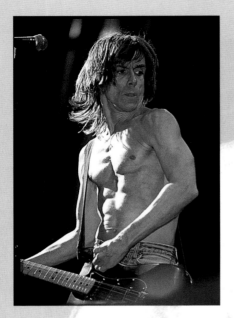

Whatever he's put it through, Iggy's body seems to have survived intact. Especially his torso (the most famous in rock history), with its fabulous definition. Iggy certainly wasn't spending his time working out in the gym, but he had the body of a scrawny bodybuilder, and, he's been known to boast, the skin of a twelve-year-old, even on the arm that took the most direct abuse from his heroin addiction.

Thin and teenage-looking, he's like an animated Scarfe Jagger, only more so. Iggy pranced and pouted, muttered with exaggerated lip and tongue movements, shook his arse, flailed his arms and legs, threw himself around, leapt into the audience and groped people, ran up and down the aisles and cursed everything in sight . . . .
Steve Peacock, *Sounds,* 1972

I'm sick of the whole rippling torso, leather and
chains animalistic narcoleptic scum-sucking hedonism
that my name got more and more submerged under.
Iggy Pop, *The Face,* 1986

At Romeo, Ig was wearing his super killer low-leather pants, and the crotch ripped during the middle of a set. The girls went bananas. Ig got a towel to cover the rip, but it fell off. One chick got bummed out and split the joint screaming. It turned out her old man was a cop, so twenty-five pigs came back to clear the joint.
Scott Asheton, *Rolling Stone,* 1970

Even if all that Iggy Pop had contributed to the history of rock performance was his penchant for self-mutilation, that alone would have been enough to guarantee him cult status, a place of pride in the alternative Rock'n'Roll Hall of Fame.

The music drives me into a peak freak. I can't feel any pain or realize what goes on around me. I'm just feeling the music and when I dive into a sea of people, it is the feeling of the music, the mood.
Iggy Pop, *Rolling Stone,* 1970

He slaps himself in the face but I think he does that for audience reaction, you know, I think he really isn't slapping himself but really slapping them and don't forget he's wearing silver lamé gloves and that's quite a different slap . . . .
Rita Redd, *Gay Power* magazine, 1971

Yeah . . . I just know for a fact that if anyone is going to be next to go, it'll be me. I'm not afraid to die. I know that sounds like a dumb boast or something, but it's a fact. I've proved it enough times, for chrissakes.
Iggy Pop, 1975

Iggy's performance style wasn't just continual motion and body abuse, there was, and is, his unmistakable voice. The perfect vehicle for Iggy to spew out his lyrics, frequently improvising, emitting the lyrics that he used to think most people weren't far out enough to understand – and he was glad.

Iggy Pop?!? . . . Musically he's so bad. I don't need to go and listen to a saw-mill all night!

Johnny Rotten, 1977

That impossibly deep, mud-caked, reverberating Grand Canyon of a Midwestern croak, purring like a Harley Davidson idling at the lights . . . .

Stephen Dalton, *NME,* 1993

I don't have to try to sound like Jim Morrison. That's the way I sound when I sing. I sing the way I feel natural singing.

Iggy, *Sounds,* 1974

Picturesque Iggy sings in a blatantly poor imitation early Jagger style. The instrumentalists sound like they've been playing their axes for two months and playing together for one month at most. The lyrics are unintelligible. Their music is loud, boring, tasteless, unimaginative and childish.
I kind of like it.

Edmund O. Ward, *Rolling Stone,* 1969

MUSICAL MOMENTS

By his own admission, the music that really got Iggy Pop motivated was the Kinks with 'You Really Got Me' and what Iggy calls the 'early, boppin' Motown', the likes of Marvin Gaye, Barrett Strong's 'Money', and Little Stevie Wonder's 'Fingertips Part One And Two'. In Rolling Stone's *review of* the Stooges' debut album, reviewer Edmund O. Ward picked up an influence of the raw energy that Ray and Dave Davies et al had brought to their early releases. Later, the Stones and the Doors had a huge impact on Iggy, as well as the Chicago blues – the Paul Butterfield Band, Junior Wells, Little Walter, Buddy Guy. He found pre-packaged pop transparent: the blues had an authentic quality. But when he first unveiled the Stooges, it was difficult to detect where the influences were: many critics found John Cale's production too classy, that the ex-Velvet had smoothed away too much of the Stooges' rough edges. The great Creem journalist Lester Bangs propounded a theory that, like the Velvet Underground who often used simple repetition as the foundation for their music, the Stooges had reduced rock music to its most basic, giving Iggy the freedom to improvise as was his wont over the top, like an avant-garde free jazz saxophonist . . . . The simplicity was of course partly out of necessity given the restricted

ability of the band: another of the legion of Stooges' myths was that when they went to Elektra Records, they had yet to write or perform an entire song, whether their own or anyone else's. Iggy could croon and keen over the driving riffs. Together they produced a sound many tried to copy but few matched, including Iggy himself as a solo artist.

I never liked that stuff made for teens – Herman's Hermits! – I saw right through it. I always aspired to be like John Lee Hooker or Muddy Waters. Those were my heroes.

Iggy Pop, Q magazine, 1988

'Fun House', the Stooges' second album, included an expanded line-up. One-time cartoonist Steve Mackay joined the band to add his tenor sax to the mix. After the controlled production of John Cale on their debut release, these sessions were an accurate reflection of the band's stage performances, recorded virtually live with a PA system in the studio.

It is as loose and raw an album as we've ever had, but every song possesses a built-in sense of intuitive taste which gives it an immediacy and propriety.

Lester Bangs, *Creem,* 1970

The title track of the Stooges' second album . . . has much in common with one of De Sade's Bastille fantasies as it has with the sexual posturing of Presley or the idiomatic sexuality of the blues. The perfect soundtrack for the end of the world bonanza.

Allan Jones, *Melody Maker,* 1974

Next to 'Grand Funk Railroad', this is the worst album I've heard this year . . . A muddy load of sluggish, unimaginative rubbish heavily disguised by electricity and called American rock. This album only goes to show up the gullible efforts of record companies, and the people who raise such groups to absurd status.

Roy Hollingworth,
Melody Maker, 1970

When I hear 'Fun House' I just think, Yeah, there's something about this one that's good. Of all my records that's the one that's got the most of me on.

Iggy Pop, *Mojo,* 1996

'Raw Power' was the Stooges' last chance for redemption. Signed to CBS after Elektra Records had unceremoniously dumped the band, Iggy and guitarist James Williamson – followed by the Asheton brothers, who were shipped in from the States when it became clear how critical they were to the sound – were sequestered in the company's London studios. There they were under the eye of David Bowie, who intervened during the production process, to the musicians' dismay. The controversy still lingers to the point that even today it is rumoured that Pop may be intending to remix the album back to the way it could have been.

Their idea of stretching out musically is something like 'LA Blues': nearly five minutes of pure cacophony that makes avantgarde jazz sound like a lullaby.

Michael Oldfield, *Melody Maker,* 1974

Snarling, amphetamine-spiked songs such as 'Your Pretty Face Is Going To Hell' and 'Search And Destroy' are dragged violently along by guitarist James Williamson's whiplash chords and Iggy's numb, misanthropic vocals, to chart a nihilistic emotional territory that a few years later Richard Hell And The Voidoids and the Sex Pistols would also explore.

Henry Williams, *Q* magazine, 1988

'Raw Power' found them as malevolent as ever, particularly on the title track, 'Search And Destroy', 'Gimme Danger', 'Shake Appeal' and 'Death Trip'. And yet . . . a certain sophistication has crept in; the raggedness that gave added bite to their first two albums is replaced by cold calculation, as though Iggy was being told: 'go berserk!'

Michael Oldfield, *Melody Maker,* 1977

When Iggy, replenished, refreshed and under Bowie's wing, came back into the limelight, he issued two solo albums within a year. It was 1977, and he had become the darling of the British punk scene, but in 'The Idiot' he delivered an album that had nothing of The Stooges' approach, a morbid, unsettling, not surprisingly autobiographical piece. Iggy had described this as his 'desperation time' – he'd either get his act together or simply disappear into the arms of oblivion.

In the place of phalanxes of the raging Stooges guitars so beloved by the punks was the mind-numbing drone of 'mekanik' rock – music as compelling as it was disturbing.
NME, 1978

It's two o'clock in the morning and I'm playing 'The Idiot' for the fifth time running. Can't stop, it's so compelling . . . but very VERY strange.
Kris Needs, *Zigzag, 1977*

No longer decadent punk, but the full-blooded scream of damnation itself. As such, it's damn unhealthy, depressing, perverse, harrowing and . . . strangely addictive. Certain, so-called Iggy fans will mutter morosely about the lack of heavy metal rock action, but that's only because they can't see that 'The Idiot' is really only the next logical step from the hell-fire tinglings of 'Raw Power' in order to keep the Pop's demon-in-residence biting back on vinyl.

Nick Kent, *NME, 1977*

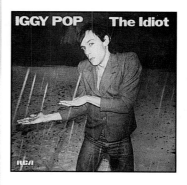

GODFATHER OF PUNK

As the British punk movement built up its irresistible head of steam through 1976 and into 1977, its luminaries sought fresh role models to counteract what they saw as the stagnant direction offered by the old farts of the rock industry. Alternative America offered the strongest potential: the new wave US bands like the Ramones, glam/trash acts like the New York Dolls. But amid the predictability and the lack of inspiration of the rest of the music scene, the inflated grandeur and the stadium pomp, one figure shone out – Iggy Stooge. He was swiftly adopted by the movement if not as its father figure then certainly as its elder brother. He and his band had already set out some of the core beliefs central to the punk manifesto. The attitude was unrepentant: a disregard for what anyone thought, a cocky pleasure in causing moral outrage, a commitment to delivering a message of alienation and anger. And the music was searingly simple – although deceptively so, since most bands who ever tried merely to copy the Stooges' sound failed miserably. One school of thought still believes that it is Stooge guitarist Ron Asheton rather than Iggy who deserves the title of punk godfather: his brute electric riff work laying the foundations for the whole punk sound. Wherever the credit was deserved, the Stooges had posthumously found a new and enthusiastic audience. Iggy might enjoy doing a wicked impression of Johnny Rotten's

interpretation of the Stooges' 'No Fun', but he respected the Pistols enough to work with both Glen Matlock and Steve Jones, although by the time of Jones's collaborations on 1986's 'Blah-Blah-Blah' and 1988's 'Instinct', the godfather was already saying that his revised lifestyle featured a spot of vacuuming, domesticated shopping trips and dinner at home. The previously high-risk Iggy was even finding he could get health insurance for the first time in his life, proof that even prototype punks can mellow and grow old disgracefully.

This album shows that Iggy was the poseur, the image and the 'heavy metal kid'! Forget Rotten for a while, you've never heard crowd/performer abuse like this, and what's so perfect is that the music is boosted by it.

Sniffin' Glue, 1976, review of 'Metallic K.O.'

There was no doubt about the punk bands's allegiance to Iggy Pop. The Pistols released 'No Fun', off the Stooges' debut album, as the B-side of their July 1977 single 'Pretty Vacant'. The Damned's own debut 'Damned Damned Damned' included a cover of 'I Feel Alright'. Every punk fanzine featured the man (including one called I Wanna Be Your Dog), and the seminal Sniffin' Glue *was Iggy-heavy by Issue Number 3. Subsequent generations would follow their lead.*

I've been an Iggy fanatic for about four years. Before I ever got 'Raw Power' I used to borrow somebody else's. I used to take the cover to bed with me. The first time I saw the Pistols last Spring they done an Iggy number and I saw 'em every week after that.

Gaye Advert of The Adverts, *Sniffin' Glue*, 1977

In the Sex Pistols' lyrics we can easily detect a perspective and style strongly reminiscent of Iggy's; their music also bears the indelible mark of The Stooges, like that of so many of their contemporaries and successors.

Ralph Traitor, *Sounds*, 1987

Unhealthy looking, sallow-skinned young peons forming bands with names like Blue In Heaven and Leather Nun attempt to stalk the same cagey precincts that Iggy Pop, the Nabob of Nihilism, once frequented, ejaculating in the self same godforsaken 'mondo' baritone about drugs, death, spent passions and the blighted scenery surrounding life's haphazard highway.

Nick Kent, *The Face,* 1986

I was sick in hospital, my pancreas blew up, I was almost dead, but Iggy's career gave me hope I could survive. Iggy, Thunders and the Pistols rule!

Duff McKagan, Guns 'N Roses

*As is the nature of his worldview, Iggy
regarded his new disciples with a
certain pride and understanding, but
he could also raise a quizzical eye.*

I started reading in the papers about me
being the 'Godfather of Punk' and I figured
well, if I'm going to be the Godfather, then
I'm going to be a real Godfather, Mafia-
style. Taking no shit from no-one and
screwing anyone who tried to screw me.
Iggy Pop

That band *walk tall*. It's like looking at
a pile of rubbish and knowing you
made it rubbish. They don't owe me
anything. I did it all for myself.
Iggy Pop, NME, 1977, on the Sex Pistols

I was behind the times when I started,
and I'm still behind the times. And you
know, looking ahead of me, at what's
in front of me, in quotes ha ha, I'm
fucking relieved I'm behind the times.
Iggy Pop, The Face, 1981

*Time moves on. Iggy turned fifty in April 1997.
Married, relatively clean, relatively relaxed, relatively
normal, he was reserving his more youthful energies
for his stage work. On the verge of becoming the
grandfather of punk, he seemed ready, like Candide,
to settle for cultivating his garden.*

You know, if I had never been into music, I'd have liked
to be a professional golfer. Some years ago I was
pretty good at golf, playing off around four handicap,
but I haven't played for two years now. One of my
roadies took my clubs to a pawn shop because I owed
him money. I think I'd have been good at anything I
tried. Maybe I could even have been the President.

Iggy, *Melody Maker,* 1973

I do a very nice steak and fries provençal. Using
a little sage. I can do the laundry pretty good.
The gardening I've now farmed out but for a
while back there I was into organic gardening.

Iggy Pop, *Q* magazine, 1996

That guy is on some other motherfucking planet,
but I dug his pants.

Audience member **Larry Piazza,** *Rolling Stone,* 1970

THE MUSIC

★★★★★   Essential listening
★★★   OK
★   Frankly, not the best!

SINGLES
Real Wild Child (Wild One)/Little Miss Emperor – November 1986 ★★★★
Candy/Pussy Power – December 1990 ★★★

ALBUMS
THE STOOGES:
The Stooges – August 1969 ★★★★
1969/I Wanna Be Your Dog/We Will Fail/No Fun/Real Cool Time/Ann/Not
Right/Little Doll
*Well, it certainly is an understatement to say that they have a marked lack of
pretension . . . They suck, and they know it, so they throw the fact back in your
face and say 'So what? We're just havin' fun.' They emit a raw energy . . . the fun
is infectious. If you want to have a real cool time, just bop on down to your local
platter vendor and pick up the Stooges' record.*
Edmund O. Ward, *Rolling Stone,* 1969

Fun House – August 1970 ★★★★★
Down On The Street/Loose/TV Eye/Dirt/I Feel Alright (1970)/Fun House/L.A. Blues
*Do you long to have your mind blown open so wide that it will take weeks for you
to pick up the little, bitty pieces? Do you ache to feel all right? Then by all means,
you simply must come visit us at the Stooges' Fun House.*
Charlie Burton, *Rolling Stone,* 1970

IGGY AND THE STOOGES:
Raw Power – May 1973 ★★★★
Search And Destroy/Gimme Danger/Your Pretty Face Is Going To
Hell/Penetration/Raw Power/I Need Somebody/Shake Appeal/Death Trip
*A classic. 'Raw Power' is infused with malevolence and Iggy's feisty wailing and
groaning. Orgasmic.*

Metallic K.O. – July 1976 ★★★
Louie Louie/Cock In My Pocket/Rich Bitch/Gimme Danger/Head On The
Curb/Raw Power
*'Metallic K.O.' is the only rock album I know where you can actually hear hurled
beer bottles breaking against guitar strings . . . Wrigglingly, obscenely alive.*
Lester Bangs, *Village Voice,* 1977

80

SOLO:

The Idiot – March 1977 ★★★★½
Sister Midnight/Nightclubbing/Funtime/Baby/China Girl/Dum Dum Boys/Tiny Girls/Mass Production
'The Idiot' . . . steeped in the so-called 'minimalist' ambience currently so fashionable amongst young bands who've spent too much time listening to Iggy and taking him seriously, is the most savage indictment of rock posturing ever recorded. 'The Idiot' is a necrophiliac's delight.
John Swanson, *Rolling Stone, 1977*

Lust For Life – September 1977 ★★★★½
Lust For Life/Sixteen/Some Weird Sin/The Passenger/Tonight/Success/Turn Blue/Neighborhood Threat/Fall In Love With Me
Probably his best, considered by many to be the definitive Pop recording. recorded and mixed in Berlin, in just 13 days, with David Bowie. 'The Passenger' was inspired by a Jim Morrison poem.

TV Eye: 1977 Live – May 1978 ★★
TV Eye/Funtime/Sixteen/I Got A Right/Lust For Life/Dirt/Nightclubbing/I Wanna Be Your Dog

New Values – May 1979 ★★★
Tell Me A Story/New Values/Girls/I'm Bored/Don't Look Down/The Endless Sea/Five Foot One/How Do Ya Fix A Broken Part/Angel/Curiosity/African Man/Billy Is A Runaway
Even if you can't feel comfortable with its vitality or you can't take it seriously then accept 'New Values' as the best album the Stones never made, and hear some of the best rock'n'roll singing ever . . . Osterberg has never been so emancipated, so invincible, so genuinely nihilistic.
Paul Morley, *NME, 1979*

Soldier – January 1980 ★★½
Loco Mosquito/Ambition/Take Care Of Me/Get Up And Get Out/Play It Safe/I'm A Conservative/Dog Food/I Need More/Knockin' Em Down/Mr. Dynamite/I Snub You

Party – June 1981 ★★★
Pleasure/Rock And Roll Party/Eggs On Plate/Sincerity/Houston Is Hot Tonight/ Pumpin' For Jill/Happy Man/Bang Bang/Sea Of Love/Time Won't Let Me
As an album, 'Party' only reached Number 166 in the US, but 'Bang Bang' became a hugely popular US dance hit.

Zombie Birdhouse – September 1982 ★★★
Run Like A Villain/The Villagers/Angry Hills/Life Of Work/Ballad Of Cookie McBride/Ordinary Bummer/Eat Or Be Eaten/Bulldozer/Platonic/The Horse Song/Watching The News/Street Crazies
After the mindless celebration of 'Party', Iggy has shaken off the hangover and come to his senses – well, what's left of them anyway. He slowly introduces the new crooning Ig, a mutant creature somewhere between Frank Sinatra and Jim Morrison.
Ian Pye, *Melody Maker,* 1982

Blah-Blah-Blah – October 1986 ★★★★
Real Wild Child (Wild One)/Baby It Can't Fall/Shades/Fire Girl/Isolation/Cry For Love/Blah-Blah-Blah/Hideaway/Winners & Losers/Little Miss Emperor
Iggy Pop is so close back to flaunting, flaming magnificence, the difference is not worth a tinker's cuss. Iggy, the true saint in sin, lashes out like he hasn't done for almost a decade.
John Wilde, *Sounds,* 1986

Instinct – July 1988 ★★★½
Cold Metal/High on You/Strong Girl/Tom Tom/Easy Rider/Power & Freedom/Lowdown/Instinct/Tuff Baby/Squarehead
Recorded with Sex Pistol Steve Jones, 'Instinct' reached Number 61 in the UK and Number 110 in the US.

Brick By Brick – August 1990 ★★★★
Home/Main Street Eyes/I Won't Crap Out/Candy/Butt Town/Pussy Power/Moonlight Lady/Something Wild/Neon Forest/Starry Night/The Undefeated/My Baby Wants To Rock And Roll/Brick By Brick/Livin' On The Edge Of The Night

With 'Brick by Brick', Iggy has completed the move from egocentric punk brat to humbly optimistic everyman philosopher, from the petulance of 'No Fun' and his concurrent self-abasement to a man with simple wishes.
Roy Wilkinson, *Sounds,* 1990

American Caesar – September 1993
★★★¹⁄₂
Character/Wild America/Mixin' The Colors/Jealousy/Hate/It's Our Love/Plastic & Concrete/Fuckin' Alone/Highway Song/Beside You/Sickness/Boogie Boy/Perforation Problems/Social Life/Louie Louie/Caesar/Girls Of N.Y.
A storming punk record . . . Iggy's new band approximate the Stooges' grungefather grandeur better than most.
Danny Frost, *NME,* 1993

'American Caesar' was Pop's first album for Virgin records, promoted by a five-day UK tour.

Naughty Little Doggie – March 1996 ★★★
I Wanna Live/Pussy Walk/Innocent World/Knucklehead/To Belong/Keep On Believing/Outta My Head/Shoeshine Girl/Heart Is Saved/Look Away
Iggy performed short tours of the US and UK to promote this latest album. After a three-year break, 'Naughty Little Doggie' provided a welcome outburst of true Iggy style. In raging, inimitable Pop mode, he exploded into a Britpop world and the audiences loved him.
Andy Gill, *Mojo,* 1996

THE HISTORY

Key Dates
21 April 1947
Born James Jewel (or Newell according to other sources) Osterberg in Muskegan, Ann Arbor, Michigan. His father James, is English, a school teacher, his American mother, Louella, an executive secretary. In pre-Iggy days is known to friends as Jimmy. The family live in a trailer park, Coachville Mobile Park, in Ypsilanti near Ann Arbor. Young James goes on to attend Pioneer High School: other alumni include Bob Seger, the Rationals, and Bill Kirchen of Commander Cody And The Lost Planet Airmen.

1963-1966
Joins local covers band – The Iguanas – as a drummer. The band turn professional in 1965 and support class acts like the Four Tops, the Marvelettes and the Shangri-Las. The Iguanas issue a limited edition single, a cover version of Bo Diddley's 'Mona' b/w 'I Don't Know Why', in August 1966.

1966
James Osterberg mutates into Iggy Pop: Iggy after the Iguanas, Pop from local dude and glue-sniffer Jim Popp. Joins rival band The Prime Movers, meets Ron Asheton and Dave Alexander. Moves to Chicago after the band folds, and after spending one semester at the University of Michigan. While in Chicago he lives in the basement of Bob Koester, owner of the Delmark label, absorbing the blues, playing with local bluesmen, including Johnny Young, Shakey Walter Horton and J. B. Hutto.

April 1967
Sees the Velvet Underground for the first time – later claims the gig, at the University of Michigan, changed his life.

October 1967
Live debut, at a local Hallowe'en party, of The Stooges, which Iggy has formed back in Michigan with Ron Asheton, Scott Asheton (Ron's brother) and Dave Alexander. Their first manager is Ron 'The Professor' Richardson, a local schoolmaster who returns to teaching once he sees what he's taken on, and the band's management is assumed by Johnny Silver, who has been at the party along with the Stooges' big brother band, MC5.

March 1968
First public performance, at the Grande Ballroom in Detroit. Early Stooges gigs from Michigan to San Francisco include Iggy getting busted in Romeo, Michigan, for indecent exposure.

September 1968
Elektra A&R man Danny Fields comes to Detroit to do a deal with MC5. They recommend he take a look at the Stooges who are playing with them at a benefit for the Children's Community School in the Union Ballroom on the University of Michigan campus. Fields, impressed, persuades Elektra to sign up the band. Humble Pie and T. Rex will both later refuse to sign with Elektra because of its association with The Stooges.

August 1969
Debut album 'The Stooges' is released (the 'Psychedelic' tag having been dropped), recorded in four days at the Hit Factory, NYC, produced by John Cale, preferred to original choice Jerry Ragavoy who had worked with Garnett Mimms and Lorraine Ellison. The line-up Iggy Stooge (vocals), Ron Asheton (guitar), Dave Alexander (bass), Scott Asheton (drums). The album reaches US Number 106. Later in the year Pop makes his movie debut in a François de Menil art-house film with German singer Nico, who has become his girlfriend. Their roles consist of waving plastic limbs around in a field of potatoes . . . .

June 1970
In the year Iggy's son Eric is born, The Stooges give a classic performance at Cincinnati Pop Festival. Iggy walks out into the audience supported by their arms. The bill also features Grand Funk Railroad, Mountain, Alice Cooper and Traffic. The show is televised, broadcast as 'A Midsummer Night's Rock'.

August 1970
Second Stooges album, 'Fun House', released, with an expanded line-up including tenor saxophonist Steve Mackay. Album produced by Don Gallucci, the keyboard player in the Kingsmen, of 'Louie Louie' fame. Lester Bangs is inspired to pen a 10,000-word review in *Creem* magazine. Bill Cheatham, one of the Stooges' roadies, joins as an additional guitarist lasting six shows. Shortly afterwards Dave Alexander is fired following a particularly disastrous performance. James Williamson joins on guitar as does another ex-roadie Zeke Zettner.

October 1970
Steve Mackay fired from The Stooges.

June 1971
Elektra concerned: about the low sales of both albums; because a number of gigs are cancelled and because Iggy is caught with an underage girl. They dispatch senior executive and producer Don Gallucci first class from New York to Ann Arbor to see if a third album is possible. Extremely disturbed by what they discover, they drop the band.

August 1971
The Stooges split up – too many drugs, line-up problems, and no label. An accident in July when the roof of their tour van is sliced off doesn't help. Iggy retires to Florida, works cutting lawns, and improves his golf. Tries to kick heroin habit.

April 1972
Meets David Bowie and his manager Tony DeFries, who persuade Iggy & The Stooges to reform and sign a management deal. Pop, the Asheton brothers and Williamson make their UK debut in July at Kings Cross Cinema, London.

May 1973
'Raw Power', including the nihilistic classic 'Search And Destroy', recorded at CBS studios in London, is released. Originally due to be Pop, Williamson and British session musicians, the Ashetons have to be flown in since no one else can handle the task. Disagreements as Pop and Williamson's mix is remixed by Bowie. Scott Thurston joins on keyboards, replacing keyboardist Robert Sheff. Williamson is sacked but later reinstated.

February 1974
The last Stooges gig takes place at the Michigan Palace, Detroit, under a barrage of missiles from the Scorpions biker gang, challenged to a face-down by Iggy. The whole extraordinary event is captured (along with an earlier October 1973 gig at the same venue) on the 'Metallic K.O.' bootleg. The Stooges finally disband.

May 1974
NME announces that Iggy will being doing a UK tour, but Pop disappears before anything is settled. He reappears at a Jim Morrison commemoration concert at LA's Whisky-A-Go-Go.

1975
After time living on the streets, Iggy becomes seriously ill and checks into an institution to get off heroin. David Bowie reputed to be Pop's only visitor. Jimmy Webb and rock journalist Bob Edmonds sponsor recording sessions for Pop with James Williamson and Scott Thurston.

March 1976
Iggy, Bowie, Bowie's bodyguard and an unnamed woman are arrested in a hotel room in Rochester, NY, after a tip-off, and charged with possession of 6oz of marijuana.

June 1976
Pop and Bowie begin work on a new Pop solo album. Later in the year both relocate to West Berlin. Recording done there and in France at the Château d'Herouville (Elton John's 'Honky Chateau'). Photographs appear in the press of Bowie and Pop in Moscow stopping off on a train journey from Switzerland to Finland where Bowie is to perform.

January 1977
Pop provides guest backing vocals on Bowie's album 'Low'.

March 1977
Signs to RCA (Bowie's label). Iggy releases 'The Idiot', produced by Bowie — the only other musician on the album, apart from Carlos Alomar (guitar). Breaks the UK Top 30 and US Top 75, and includes 'China Girl', later a hit for Bowie. Tours with Bowie on keyboards and supported by Blondie. Bowie overcomes his fear of flying to fly for the first time in six years to support Iggy. Ron Wood and Bill Wyman plus wives turn up to watch one of the shows.

MoDERN iCoNS — IGGY POP

May 1977
A UK reissue of 'Raw Power' makes the UK Top 50.

September 1977
'Lust For Life' released. Recorded in Berlin, it includes 'The Passenger', inspired by Jim Morrison, and features the Sales brothers on bass and drums, with Bowie on piano.

April 1979
After a move to Arista, Pop gets a band together with Thurston, Glen Matlock, and Jackie Clark (from the Ike & Tina Turner band), but various problems with the authorities mean a number of dates are cancelled – for example, they are banned from Dunstable because the local council is unhappy with Glen Matlock's presence.

October 1979
Release of 'New Values', produced by James Williamson; subsequent tour includes Glen Matlock on bass.

September 1982
'Zombie Birdhouse' released on Chris Stein's Animal label. Blondie drummer Clem Burke also on the album. Pop and Stein produce the soundtrack for the movie *Rock'n'Rule*.

October 1982
Publishes *I Need More: The Stooges and Other Stories*, written with Anne Wehrer. Later reissued by Henry Rollins's publishing house, 2.13.61 Publications.

December 1982
Sprains ankle in Canada, forced to cancel four shows, but appears in San Francisco with gaffer tape bound round the ankle.

June 1983
Bowie's version of 'China Girl' reaches number 2 in the UK singles charts.

1984
Marries Suchi, who he met on a tour of Japan. Supplies the title song for Alex Cox's *Repo Man*, and appears the following year in *Sid And Nancy*. Other movie

and TV work includes *The Color Of Money*, John Waters's *Cry-Baby*, *Miami Vice* and Jim Jarmusch's *Dead Man* and *City Of Angels*.

October 1986
The album 'Blah-Blah-Blah' (Pop is now on A&M) is generally deemed to mark a return to form.

November 1986
Pop's cover version of 'Real Wild Child', first recorded by Australian rock'n'roll pioneer Johnny O'Keefe in 1957, cracks the UK Top 10.

July 1988
Australian Au-Go-Go label releases a double album of Stooges' covers called 'Hard To Beat: 21 Stooges Killers' including tributes by God, Raw Power, The Seminal Rats and The Hard-Ons.

July 1990
'Brick By Brick' released (produced by Don Was), including Guns 'N Roses' Slash and Duff McKagan.

January 1991
Duets with Debbie Harry on Cole Porter's 'Well Did You Evah' on the AIDS benefit album 'Red Hot + Blue'.

August 1991
Headlines the first day at the Reading festival, with a support line-up including Nirvana, Babes In Toyland, Dinosaur Jr., Silverfish and Sonic Youth.

July 1993
The album 'American Caesar' released on Virgin Records.

July 1994
Performs at the Phoenix festival.

March 1996
'Naughty Little Doggie' released. In interviews at the time Iggy suggests that he may be planning to reform the Stooges with the two Asheton brothers.

THE CAST

Dave Alexander. Born 3 June 1947, Ann Arbor, Michigan. Knows Ron Asheton from school and their first band the Dirty Shames. Joins the Stooges and moves to bass for their first public performance. Plays on 'The Stooges' and 'Fun House', but is replaced by Zeke Zettner in 1970 after a bad gig performance. Drink rather than drugs is his downfall: he dies February 1975 in Detroit.

Ron Asheton. Born 17 July 1948, Washington DC. A friend of Dave Alexander in Ann Arbor: the two drop out of high school and go on a trip to England, catching The Move and The Who live, impressed by Pete Townshend's destruction of yet another guitar. Fails to get a permanent place in the Prime Movers despite Iggy's help (he's too rock'n'roll), so joins Scott Richardson in a band called the Chosen Few. When that band breaks up, Iggy phones and invites him to join the Stooges. Ron plays bass at the first gig, then moves to guitar for the next. Famous for the range of Nazi uniforms he employs for stage wear. Plays bass and guitar on all three Stooges' albums. Dave Marsh writes 'Ron's guitar playing embodies the Stooges' music. What he is doing is learning how to control the electric guitar. With emphasis on the *electric*.' After the Stooges split he is the only one of Pop's cohorts to maintain any significant profile in the music industry, forming The New Order (six years ahead of their UK indie namesake) with Scott, then moves on to Destroy All Monsters with ex-MC5 bassist Michael Davis. They release a single 'Bored' in 1978 and some private EPs. Finally forms New Race with ex-MC5 drummer Dennis Thompson. Still lives in Ann Arbor.

Scott Asheton. Born 16 August 1949, Washington DC. Younger brother of Ron. Taught the rudiments of drumming by Iggy, he plays throughout the Stooges' career. Signs of his own personal unravelling include being at the wheel of the tour van in July 1971 when he tries to negotiate a 12 foot bridge with the 16 foot high van; selling off his drum kit to score drugs (even Iggy notices when Scott has to perform with the bass drum and precious little else). Also develops theory on final 1973 tour that never changing his clothes will bring him closer to God. Little musical activity after the Stooges, surfacing in Ron's The New Order and Sonic's Rendezvous Band with Fred 'Sonic' Smith of MC5, but mainly returns to obscurity in Ann Arbor.

David Bowie. Meets Iggy in April 1972 at a party thrown by record company RCA at Max's Kansas City, NYC. At the time Bowie is on a roll: aggressively promoted by Tony DeFries, who has replaced Bowie's manager Kenneth Pitt, a handsome deal has been struck with RCA and 'The Rise And Fall Of Ziggy Stardust' is about to be released. Bowie is in full flow. Bowie arranges for Pop, who is in limbo following the Stooges' firing from Elektra, to be signed up with MainMan, Bowie's management company, and Pop is signed to CBS. The recording sessions for the third Stooges' album 'Raw Power' are overseen by Bowie, who re-mixes the original production by Pop and James Williamson, not to everyone's satisfaction. When Pop reaches the depths again, Bowie, who has revealed a Midas touch when it comes to production, reviving the career of Lou Reed, for example, comes to his rescue again, taking Pop on tour, working on his new solo albums, and remaining a regular influence throughout the rest of Pop's career. In 1983 Bowie's single success with their song 'China Girl' brings Iggy a much-needed income stream.

John Cale. The Welsh-born Cale, after studying viola and keyboards at Goldsmiths College in London, goes out to the States on a scholarship to the Eastman Conservatory in Massachusetts. From there he gravitates to New York, meets Lou Reed, and joins the Velvet Underground, playing with the band until 1968. Moving into production, he oversees Nico's solo efforts and is chosen to produce the Stooges' debut album, which he completes shortly before the release of 'Vintage Violence' in 1970, the first album of his long solo career.

Nico. The thirty-year-old German actress/singer meets Iggy when she goes to the New York studio where Velvets' colleague John Cale is working with the Stooges on their debut album. Iggy is nineteen and enjoys an exotic and erotic adventure with her. Pop claims she introduced him to three things: Dante's 'Inferno', Beaujolais and oral sex (though, in contradictory sources, Pop also claims to have been a virgin until the age of twenty when he was seduced by a woman of twenty five). Through Nico, Iggy makes his first (never released) film appearance in an art movie. He writes the song 'We Will Fall', which appears on the first album, for her — it is considered one of the worst songs The Stooges recorded.

Other sidemen on Pop's solo albums include ex-Rundgren band members **Tony Sales** (bass) and **Hunt Sales** (drums) who later work with David Bowie in Tin Machine, **Fred 'Sonic' Smith** (guitar, ex-MC5), **Jackie Clarke** (bass, ex-Ike and Tina Turner), **Klaus Kreiger** (drums, ex-Tangerine Dream). **Glen Matlock** (bass, ex-Sex Pistols), **Steve Jones** (guitar, also ex-Pistols), **Barry Andrews** (keyboards, ex-XTC), **Paul Garristo** (drums, ex-Psychedelic Furs), **Slash** and **Duff McKagan** (guitar and bass, Guns 'N Roses). Name producers include Bowie's, **Don Was** and Blondie's **Chris Stein**.

Other Stooges. Steve Mackay, tenor sax player, previously a cartoonist for *Detroit's Death Comix*, joins for 'Fun House', but is sacked in October 1970. Sits in on drums for The Stooges in 1971 when Scott crashes the tour van. Widely reported to have OD'd, he is in fact still alive and kicking. **Bob Sheff**, keyboard player, replaced by Scott Thurston, had played with Iggy in The Prime Movers back in the early days. He is now an avant-garde composer going by the name Blue 'Gene' Tyranny. **Scott Thurston** joins on keyboards for the final 1973 tour; works with Pop on 'Lust For Life' and is retained to 1979 playing on 'TV Eye Live' and 'New Values', before joining The Motels. In the Nineties he is a member of Tom Petty's touring band. **Zeke Zettner**, roadie upgraded to guitar in 1970, and in turn replaced, dies in 1975.

James Williamson. Having met Ron Asheton in The Chosen Few, is brought in to replace guitarist Bill Cheatham in 1970. Nicknamed 'The Skull' he is the only genuine bad boy Stooge, having done time in reform school for taking cars and speed. Assumes musical leadership pre-'Raw Power', playing lead and rhythm guitar. Sacked after Bowie and DeFries take over but asked to rejoin for final tour. After the Stooges, works on 'Kill City' as Iggy Pop & James Williamson, producing that album as well as Pop's 1979 'New Values'. Becomes an LA-based recording engineer and gets involved in the Silicon Valley computing industry.

THE BOOKS

I Need More – Iggy Pop (2.13.61) 1982, reissued 1996
The Lives And Crimes Of Iggy Pop – Mike West, 1982
Iggy Pop: The Wild One – Per Nilsen and Dorothy Sherman, 1988

PICTURE CREDITS

Pages 2-3 Michel Linssen/Redferns. **Page 5** Andy Catlin/London Features International (LFI). **Page 8** Michel Linssen/Redferns. **Page 10** Ebet Roberts/Redferns. **Page 11** Ian Dickson/Redferns. **Page 12** Ebet Roberts/Redferns. **Page 13** LFI. **Page 14** Preston, Kent, Levine/LFI. **Page 15** Andy Kent/LFI. **Page 16** Steve Rapport/LFI. **Page 17** Janet Macoska/LFI. **Page 18** Michel Linssen/Redferns. **Page 19** Michel Linssen/Redferns. **Page 20** Michel Linssen/Redferns. **Page 21** Michael Ochs Archives/Redferns. **Page 22** Paul Cox/LFI. **Page 23** Des Willie/Redferns. **Page 25** (l) Andy Catlin/LFI; (r) Mick Hutson/Redferns. **Page 26** LFI. **Page 29** (t) Kevin Mazur/LFI; (b) Andy Kent/LFI. **Page 30** (tl) Courtesy of RCA Records; (tr) Des Willie/Redferns; (b) Steve Rapport/LFI. **Page 33** (l) Preston, Kent, Levine/LFI; (r) Ebet Roberts/Redferns. **Page 34** Ebet Roberts/Redferns. **Page 35** Erica Echenberg/Redferns. **Pages 36-7** (t) Michael Ochs Archives/Redferns; (b) Michael Ochs Archives. **Page 37** Ebet Roberts/Redferns. **Page 38** Geoff Swaine/LFI. **Page 41** Erica Echenberg/Redferns. **Pages 42-3** Paul Cox/LFI. **Page 45** Michael Ochs Archives/Redferns. **Page 46** (t) Patrick Ford/Redferns; (b) Richie Aaron/Redferns. **Page 49** (l) Clouds Studios/LFI; (r) Paul Cox/LFI. **Page 51** (l) LFI; (r) Michael Ochs Archives/Redferns. **Page 53** (l) Ian Dickson/Redferns; (r) LFI. **Page 54** Ebet Roberts/Redferns. **Page 55** Ebet Roberts/Redferns. **Page 56** (t) Richie Aaron/Redferns; (bl) Michel Linssen/Redferns; (br) Ian Dickson/Redferns. **Page 58** (t) Mick Hutson/Redferns; (b) Michel Linssen/Redferns. **Page 60** Michel Linssen/Redferns. **Page 61** Michel Linssen/Redferns. **Page 63** (t) Suzi Gibbons/Redferns; (b) Michel Linssen/Redferns. **Page 65** Ian Davies/Redferns. **Page 66** Ian Dickson/Redferns. **Page 67** Janet Macoska/LFI. **Page 68** (t) Glenn A. Baker Archives/Redferns; (b) Courtesy of CBS Records. **Page 69** Glenn A. Baker Archives/Redferns. **Pages 70-1** (t) Preston, Kent, Levine/LFI; (b) Richie Aaron/Redferns. **Page 71** Courtesy of RCA Records. **Page 73** Michel Linssen/Redferns. **Page 75** (t) LFI; (b) Richie Aaron/Redferns. **Page 76** Richie Aaron/Redferns. **Page 77** Richie Aaron/Redferns. **Page 79** (tl) Des Willie/Redferns; (tr) Des Willie/Redferns; (b) Gems/Redferns. **Page 80** Glenn A. Baker Archives/Redferns. **Page 81** LFI. **Page 82** Ebet Roberts/Redferns. **Page 83** Michel Linssen/Redferns. **Page 84** Ebet Roberts/Redferns. **Page 88** Clouds Studios/LFI. **Page 89** Clouds Studios/LFI. **Page 91** Kevin Mazur/LFI. **Page 92** Michael Ochs Archives/Redferns. **Pages 94-5** Michel Linssen/Redferns.

Every effort has been made to contact copyright holders.
If any ommisions do occur the publisher would be
delighted to give full credit in subsequent reprints and editions.